Rollercoaster

Poems by
Ken Eaton-Dykes

Published by Ken Eaton-Dykes
Publishing partner: Paragon Publishing, Rothersthorpe
First published 2019
© Ken Eaton-Dykes 2019

ISBN 978-1-78222-703-8

Book design, layout and production management by Into Print
www.intoprint.net
+44 (0)1604 832149

In Loving Memory of My Son
Michael Eaton-Dykes
2nd February 1963 – 14th November 2018
Guitarist - Musician - Legend
Gone But Never Forgotten

PREFACE

SUDDENLY realising I wouldn't be living for ever after a bout of man flu left me pondering life on the other side. Thought to myself I must come up with the most inspiring piece of wisdom ever written, with a future destined to be quoted more often than happy birthday was ever sung, but after months of agonising, during sleepless nights I dumped the idea deciding in its stead to be content as a best seller.

GREAT GRAND KIDS

This poem is a sentimental little verse about two little girls who happen to be my great grandchildren. Have you noticed the older one gets, beside learning about the basic aspects of life, you find during that passage of time, each aspect is ever more a pixillated mass of implication to be interpreted as best you can, and passed on for the well being of your less experienced successors?

Each grinning sit astride my old rheumatic knees
a pair of exuberant saplings
aged just four rings and three
two new babes born in the woods
impatiently broke from swelling buds
off a sturdy family tree

roots mulched firm bedded deep
fed by antecedents in their everlasting sleep
flourishing, fixed, to a healthy mix
of assorted ancestry.

Untiring, unbridled, undaunted, unfearing,
wide eyed, so cute, delightful, endearing
escaped to the sky from the dappled dark clearing
dazzling arrays of new things to be gleaning.
Halting enquiries launch life's learning curve
curiosity heightens, hard wired verve

"Why was Jack Horner sat in a corner
with an enormous pie?"
"why was Mary quite contrary?"
eyes demand an instant reply
He was looking for somewhere to put his thumb
maybe find and eat a delicious plum
I return with a wearisome sigh

From small beginnings we learn to fly
some find it a struggle
but succeed by and by
Shy, meek, outgoing, mild,
geeky, reserved, or outrageously wild
Be patient, be gentle, think love is all.

There's no growing wrong
only upward and strong
from pools of sweet memory
imbided on recall.

Just when your children's children have blossomed into *what you hope* are successful responsible adults, is it a time to take stock of your relationships worth? and together strengthened with the benefit of hindsight, look back on and agree it was time well spent. But now has evolved into a quiet, slightly boring, unproductive, not much going on, fallow period between generation building.

Then what do you know! along in rapid succession a third crop of great grandchildren arrive for us their great grandparents to again search out and dust the many books of nursery rhymes and fairy tales we had sung and recited to their excited, and equally eager to learn predecessors.

Plus the oft' repeated instance when three year old's finished rawling on your knee, sit motionless concentrating wide eyed, unblinking, intently contemplating your once young hairy nostrils.

Then suddenly perking up, they dismiss the image to the backs of their curiosity sated minds, for retrieval as a vague recollection, during future moments of Deja vu.

THE END TO A PERFECT WAY

This is how I imagine someone – say for instance a faithful old servant – after following a life of shadowy deference would prepare for the minimum inconvenience to his master. Post the casting of his mortal coil.

I've tried to please,
put others at ease
went out of my way to be friendly
clean smart warm of heart
innovative, regarded as *trendy*.
Heard New Year Day chimes eighty eight times
been subject to four different Monarchs
heard George the fifth, do the first Christmas speech
and MPs' disingenuous bollocks.

Unaccomplished, pleasant of mind
academically non inclined
a pragmatic logical thinker.
Able, efficient, do things without fuss
So *if* life's an exam...I'll get a B plus

Each night I bathe, drink a large glass of wine
don a white dressing gown purchased online
the best of material, trimmed with black.
from the finest tailor bespoken.

Climb onto bed, bones protest with a crack
hands crossed on chest, lying still on my back
a position I've trained to hold steady.
Then if I'm taken, during the night.
They'll find me laid out. Oven ready.

And so is put to rest yet another introvert serf, modelled by
DNA and inclined (gene wise) to be a hand rag for his betters.

A bad enough end you might think, but really not such a
poor fate when compared to the infinite variety of imperfect
genetical permutations with which significant numbers of
our present society are unfortunately infected, leading them
eventually into displaying unspeakable evils of varying intensity,
by way of natural tendencies inherited from an ancestry rich in
psychotic antecedents.

"What's an antecedent Sir?"
"Jones! If you only knew of the many occasions you have
sooooo nearly been one."

REMEMBERING THE HOLOCAUST

Honouring Holocaust victims
on the evening of last Monday week
reliving unspeakable horrors
through articulate rhyme and speech
we were made aware and reminded
listening silent in mournful array
those despicable thoughts
fired by hate long ago
lurk latent in hearts still today.

Awakened from restive slumber
"New Order" perverted beliefs
will repeat old agendas, long term aims
virulent hatred, fills vacuous brains
reviving the dream, inflicting the pain
death on the street,
cruel fair-haired elite

Fervent desciples sow tainted seed
threshed from rich harvests of dogmatized creed
engineered with aforethought intention
to inflame once benign, now possessed open minds
into acts, of inhuman aggression.

Smother the blazing incitements
igniting impassioned breasts.
extinguish the source of misleading news
divisive rhetoric, perverted views
these blinkered malefactors profess.

For only sincere, altruistic love
will Malevolence.
Forever, suppress.

The long cycle of the nineteen thirties generation is rapidly bringing to completion its temporary task of being trusted with the overall welfare of the planet and that of its population. But instead of using this precious time united as one voice to achieve social cohesion through fair trade, it is still being used as in the previous two centuries, insidiously by unscrupulous political leaders and businessmen for the deliberate exploitation of politically naive leaders in underdeveloped countries to their nefarious advantage with "in the beginning" enticement with bags of salt, followed by a mixture of veiled threats, and two-faced diplomacy. Backed up by the silhouette of a gun boat on the horizon.

Hatred toward the atrocity led policies from the past three centuries continues to echo from out the still open sores of yester-year conflicts.

Instead of uniting together, prospering nations competing for trade ultimately chose to face each other in violent confrontation, when broken treaties and ignored threats ripened into war, and not the handshaking sincere honest co-operation needed to build an internationally controlled peaceful future for a World where all of humanity would be equal in every respect, and minorities not graded for special treatment.

WE REMEMBER THE KILLING.
BUT FORGET THE FUTILITY OF IT

Sunday 3rd. September is the anniversary of the beginning of WW2 which left EIGHTY FIVE MILLION people dead. This piece contains personal memories of that time, plus a few thoughts on events up to the present; where we all take for granted and do not appreciate the much higher standards of living enjoyed today. The hard lessons learned from the past are long forgotten and the European Community born out of that conflict is threatened with a return to the dis-unity of those times that helped spawn the tragedies of World Wars one and two.

There will never be peace in the world. But we can at least TRY to minimise the likelihood of war, by patiently, from small beginnings, working toward global unification.

War's over and finished, an age since it started.
Was a nine year old nipper when Chamberlain imparted
that World War Two, he'd reluctantly started
"We won't let our friends the Polish people down"
he declared through a worried of the consequences frown.
Church bells were stilled into silence, that warm September day
till the end of that obscene, six year bloody affray.

It's May forty five, I'm a grubby adolescent
much bigger than Mum, obnoxious, unpleasant
not the same person when Father had gone
battling the Germans in nineteen forty one.

Mum was worried, felt sorry for her,
but perked up when she saw
as I ate my breakfast toast
the blue edged airmail letter among the morning post.
Later after school sitting down to tea
reopening the envelope she read out loud to me
what I thought exciting fun, the things our dad had seen and done,
driving a lorry, cleaning his gun
how he missed family, especially me and mum.

Ended with love and kisses, I clear the cups and then
try to guess, what's beneath the bits,
blacked out by the censor's pen.
Mum re-folds the letter, eyes glistened moist with tears
shed for the man she hadn't seen, in four long lonely years.

Now I've lived a long life and made up me mind
that the world is a constant production line,
of babies some bouncing their future assured,
a few arrive faulty, racked with pain
bearing the sins, still taking the blame
from a past indiscreet libertine's moment of shame
born to die young, a few years of age
ink barely dried, on church registry page.

Naturally selected, the healthy ones then
go on to accomplish, their three score and ten.

Husbands, mothers, siblings and others
aunties, uncles, the rich on the hill
lowly of station or ruling a nation.
When all's said and done, they're just *"grist t' mill"*

The last generation, fought and died for their nation
and from war weary Europe, a bloody gestation
produced hope in the shape of a new federation
to lessen the chance of new wars and their cause,
freedom of movement on borderless shores
But memory short, war forgotten, outdated,
short sighted fools, rising rampant with hatred
vote to destroy the goodwill created
internet xenophobes express extreme views
poisoning minds with misleading news
screaming for all but indigenous brits
to pack their bags, exit the doors
from recurrent hostile, once welcoming shores.

Raised voices in violent discourse
splits divides and trends
toward argument between family
resentment in faithful old friends.

Conducted by blinkered resurgents,
ignorance once again roars.
retrospectively, for the emergence
of perfection without any flaws
a eugenically bred, fair of head
Imperial conquering force.

When war was eventually declared I was fortunate to have been nine years old, an age mercifully when kids are lacking in worldly experience and aware only of their own personal selfish needs, no matter how petty. At that period my mind was totally insulated against any sort of sympathy toward others no matter how great a trauma they may have suffered. I was, I suppose too young as yet to have developed an empathic side to my character, and mentally incapable of expressing sympathy for others in their hour of grief.

My mother for instance.

I didn't realise the amount of stress she suffered, the years of separation from Dad along with the worry for his safety, which manifested itself in the nervous rash lasting the rest of her life. The nights spent in Aunty Nell's air raid shelter during the blitz, Grandma could be heard from next door in Aunty Elsie's shelter, hysterically crying above the cacophony of anti aircraft fire and exploding bombs. Whilst I lay drowsily unperturbed, gazing at the flickering candle's ever widening sooty stain on the concrete ceiling.

Christmas Eve nineteen forty four I'm almost fifteen. Hitler has a last go at the Manchester area launching V1 flying bombs from over the North sea. Most explode harmlessly over a wide area, but one lands in Oldham killing nearly forty civilians just weeks away from the end of hostilities.

My first shot of adrenalin had arrived, with empathy close on its heels.

A POEM OF MASS DESTRUCTION

The transmitting of hysteria by way of poetry in the hands, say of an unsuccessful writer, mind twisted with years of failure and bent on revenge against audiences skinny with the kudos, could have a devastating effect on the behaviour of gatherings large and small. This next piece describes the possible consequences:

We walk through life on our chosen track
to influence our peers, make indelible impact
My ambition as poet is to write and persistently dwell
on soul destroying stanzas that over and over regaled
will convince the listening audience how horribly they've failed.

In the beer fumed friendly ambience
of the pub on a warm Sunday night
deserved success will be mine at last, here on the open mic.
With an air of supreme confidence
giving it my very best go
smiling faces crumble to the pessimistic flow.
The audience sitting mesmerised, is putty in my palm
little do they realise there's malice in my charm
I could tell from long drawn faces, unsmiling and morose
the climax to my solo spot, was coming to a close.

Fulfillment of the master plan, this fanatical ambition
delivery of the final line, brings my life's work to fruition
swaying uncontrollably, the crowd as one react
by jumping out the window
spellbound in a suicide pact.

Revenge is so sweet. After years of ridicule meted out by unappreciative morons who could never recognise a natural genius. My only personal disappointment suffered on the night was having to cut the evening short thus saving the assembled, doomed, cultureless punters further expense at the bar of this fantastically depressing, astronomically high priced, colourless venue.

NEW YEAR RESOLUTIONS

Every year after the party season people use the beginning of this period as an easy to remember starting point from which they've pledged to banish an accumulation of dodgy vices, life threatening or otherwise, out of their everyday existence. But with very few lacking the determination to see them through. This poem contrary to the usual outcome is the story of one middle aged individual scared into success.

Christmas over, good cheer gone stale
cause and effect drinking beer by the pail
cards with good wishes still lie on the mat
can't pick them up, am *too f'kin fat.*

Sluggish lethargic toxin polluted
oversized arse in the armchair well rooted
from high flying flows, to miserable ebbs
smell like a vat of last New Year eve's dreggs

Feel rough in the morning sickly and pale
letterbox rattles with incoming mail
shaven, showered, heave myself on the scale
a peep over stomach, brings pitiful moan
read out announces, eighteen 'n' half stone.
Impressive, imposing, when one's six foot three
barrel of lard, if your short arsed like me

Really went over the top last year
abused meself with all sorts of gear
to get back in shape, inexpensive solution
I tried an intensive, New Year resolution
it's for a long time, and I'm not all that keen.
But been told if I don't
"Won't see Christmas Eighteen"

Enrolled at the Gym and on waddling in
introduce me to Stan 'the man with a plan'
to eradicate poundage, get back fit and thin
starts in with a pep talk, "So important to win"
catalogues fat bits, and when to begin

Quarter pound ear lobes, eyes sunken and hid
to expose each again, needs a lipo-sucked lid.
It takes twelve months, on salads and gherkins
to restore firm flat six packs
from nine gallon firkins.
Determined, single minded,
strict adherence, to instruction
will invigorate vitality
toned muscle construction.

Thank God it's over, wasn't much fun
tempting smells from the chippie
I'd resisted and won
I've lost so much weight, I'm in fact really thin

through unstinting hard graft, and will power
and to stay this way, exercise every day
Running round.
To get wet in the shower.

A threat to one's health caused by excesses of the good things
in life, is the inescapable make your mind up time as to your
future choice of lifestyle. Will it be the short sweet continuation
of the "Have a nice day, keep the bed sores away" Early Death
Bed Plan. Overweight riddled with type two diabetes.

Or the long (Heathly Decline Plan) alternative, "With more
Springs to enjoy" But unlike the short-term plan. This one
comes with an extra time bonus to enjoy the sleepless nights
plagued with worry regarding the dwindling sufficiency of
your pension pot.

CLOSET MISOGYNIST *(The ballad of)*

This is a sad tale concerning a young man without friends and the confidence to approach girls. Who after constant rejection by the opposite sex plans to kidnap then enslave one. But being shy, lacking in confidence, and afraid to carry out his plan. Vents his anger on an Internet downloaded, dis-embodied mechanical female voice. Alexa

Girls snigger to each other, avoiding my advances
when I sidle up with outdated lines
at the local disco dances.
They think I'm a wimp, an excruciating bore.
Whirling round, making shapes,
on the drink and sweat stained floor.
Disco finished, nearly dawn,
downhearted, dispairing, feeling forlorn.
Key opens front door with a welcoming click,
quick glance in the mirror as I pass down the hall
sees me creased and untidy, don't resemble at all,
that exuberant, sweet smelling, hunk of meat
who some hours before had took to the street
looking for love to a garage-house beat

I'm not so good looking,
dim witted, bit thick,
and the chickens fell off me shishkabob stick.

Introverted, never been kissed,
left off everyone's party list,
zero plus in self esteem.
And the buzz words used to reference me on the bustling cool
street scene, speak of an:
"Inexperienced no nothing lanky, Never had a girl,
Gobshite Mancy"
In the face of such blatant disregard,
I'm a furious hopeless contender,
consumed with a nagging burning desire
for revenge on the opposite gender.

So I Google Amazon, then hatch a plot,
wire up the house with Echo Spots.
And on starting my evil agenda, throw the switch …
The Apps spring to life.
Enslaving that smug bitch – *Alexa.*
I begin with the tunes, forty million all told,
from one hit wonders, through to those that got gold.
Elvis, Sinatra, old groaner Bing, Cliff Richard, New Order,
Dean Martin, and Sting.
In quick succession I order her play,
she's had no rest "at all" since a week yesterday.
But what's gone wrong, the plot's in crisis?
It's me that's getting the laryngitis.

I insult her, demean her, shriek that she's lazy,
neighbours must think I'm mad, or gone crazy.
But she never *ever* fails to come back.
Composed, fresh as a daisy.

Press on regardless not a minute's respite,
make her flush the bog, when I take a John Bright.
My constant reminder, *"girls are incomplete males"*
According to Aristotle. Finally flips her over the edge
with gargantuan loss of her bottle.

Now I've brought to cessation my burning obsession,
having done a magnificent job.
I knew I was getting my own back
when I sensed a submissive sob.
And to confirm this glorious victory
"elimination of irrational fear"
was the Echo Spot's silent rusting
in the puddles
of Alexa's tears.

No longer afraid of women, I'm a misogynist mister big
A chest swollen, proud to be outed
Supremacist Chauvinist **PIG**.

Well not quite the complete Chauvinist pig I'd like to be, I still go red in the face, even when I'm by myself till I swill it away with a few pints of five per-cent proof wife beating mixture. While shouting taunts about the unfair pay gap between men's and women's earnings, and all the other hurtful things I can think of, that could possibly make girls cry.

THE BREXIT BLUES

Did rich Brexiteers - the likes of Jacob Reece Mogg - put up a smoke-screen of "more money for the NHS" to conceal the real motives for dumping the EU? For instance, knowing Brexit would give them more opportunities for higher returns on their portfolio of investments, free from EU restriction? Give them also the opportunity of high returns, by asset stripping what would be newly deregulated EU protected areas of natural resources for short term gain. Should MPs be debarred from Parliament for having industrial investments of any kind if those investments depend on Government influence for their prosperity? Even royalty has - or had - money invested in the ruthless exploitive money lending (sharks) Brighter Homes, previously known as Crazy George furnishers, to partially maintain their luxury lifestyles from the obscene interest rates wrung from the poorest in British society, by way of the Brighter Homes rent to buy racket.

It's twenty one months since the vote for autonomy
unentangling ourselves from the E.U. economy
free, at last, new trade deals to seek,
plus saving one third of a billion each week.
A brilliant future together we face
on a twenty per cent meagre, industrial base?

Cheap goods come and go on Korean made shipping
Footsie one hundred's sky high and no dipping
raising false hope, for sustained prosperity.
Imports are paid for in shrinking assets
and "hired out" numeric dexterity.

Alongside cooking the company books, for conglomerate grandees
we sell our unique world renowned, financial expertise
to oppressive corrupt governments in power overseas.
Charity turned to dollars for exceptional large fees.
Then have them re-invest it into pre-assigned devices
selling chunks of London off to criminal franchises.
Many of whom have shady links
arming the murderous ISIS.

Monies stolen from funding,
intended to soothe Third World pain.
Shows up returned, as an honest earned?
above-board, Market gain.

Some of these gangsters buy football clubs,
and are really well established
living abroad, leading luxury lives
chauffeurs and flunkies serve glamourous wives.
Running ill-gotten empires, with email and faxes.
It's champagne each day, leaving us here to pay.
The shortfall in lost UK taxes.

Worlds away from their countrymen's plight,
the diseased, unemployed, food famished.
Money donated, for the poor of all ages
crookedly cleaned in a series of stages.
Finds its way back to pay footballers' wages.

From the trillions distributed round the world
we see a scandalous painting unfurled
entitled THEFT OF FUNDS AWARDED.
Millions lavished on real estate
and Premier League centre forwards.

Britain's "We Do All The Currencies"
slick Financial Team
the metaphorical only one made, "British washing machine"
will launder your money as a matter of course
clean like a whistle, no paper-trailed source.
Strong plastic tenners and rubbery fivers
guarantee us top placed "Free Market" survivors.

The decision to leave Europe, in panic-stricken haste
was not from careful reasoning, but intolerance of race.
It will take a generation to revive our failing nation
recover from the consequence of rash voting's devastation.
Plus, innumerable anomalies will show as wasted time
during which there's likely to be
run-away inflation ... instability.
No money left in the Chancellor's purse
bogged down, derailed, off line.
Let's face it folks – there's no plan B.
WE'VE ADVANCED THE WEST'S DECLINE.

Since I wrote the above despairing whine, my respect for the British establishment, and especially the managers of it – the MPs (Manipulative Pricks) – has plunged to a dangerous level after watching our unscripted leaders on TV appearing to not quite know what they were talking about when competing for the vacant Prime Ministership. As noisy confused argument supported with lots of arm waving, degenerated into (can't think of anything to say) silent arm waving, we, the watching public, suddenly realised, these clowns are no better than us, that we need to stay in the EU and hope against hope being lost in a larger assembly might eventually encourage our lot to piss facing in the same direction as Angela Merkel, to the strains of "Ode To Joy".

YOU'RE NOT HALF THE MAN HE WAS

Tears can have far reaching effects, even for those lucky enough not to have been emotionally affected by the death of a close relative in times of war.

This poem beside being just another angle on remembrance day, exposes the possible consequential years of unhappiness on marrying the recently war widowed.

At the eleventh hour, on the eleventh day,
of the eleventh month, in mournful array
under skeletal trees, on last summer's leaf
thousands of faces, in sombre relief
display circumstancially, countenanced grief.

Lugubrious music will coax mouths to pray
round a poppy strewn plinth at eleven today
and honour by way of a well worn agender
a body count up since a year last November

Contrived euphemistic rhetoric
amplified from a mitred head
conjures up a mental picture,
of smiley faces on the dead.

Imploring us remember, in two short minutes recall,
heroes who suffered the ultimate, sacrificed their all.
Inclusive of those, who raped, ravaged,
killed innocent kids, via collateral damage

The winds of time sighing by,
first cool, stem, then gently dry
tear stained cheeks, sore widowed eyes

She watches TV, "remarried"
heart scarred, but with time will repair,
devoted second husband
ill at ease in his favourite chair
feels resurgent annual jealousy
seeing tears she cannot hide
for her posthumous soldier first love,
cruelly denied

He waits, and hopes fading memory
will stop, then dry falling tears
bring to an end the mourning
blighting their union's first years.
As the flames carried high for her hero
flicker then finally dim
she might unlock the door to his love with her heart
at last, devoted to him.

History tells me that all wars are completely unnecessary as
their final results definitely do not justify the huge financial
outlay involved, or the devastating incalculable human suffering
of idiots marching to their deaths, singing *"I've got sixpence"*
after assuring loved ones confidently that
"…it'll be all over by Christmas".

IT'S A WONDERFUL WORLD (OR IS IT?)

Being born is a most traumatic experience. Pulled and pushed into a cruel world of exploitation. A world where from day one in order to survive, we have to spend each twenty-four hour period being hardened off and de-sensitized tackling the innumerable daily challenges thrown up as we stumble through this euphemistically disguised vale of tears. On the difficult to navigate yellow brick road to experience.

In a tiny corner of the Milky Way
just before dawn at break of day
inside a room under star-lit skies
lubricated by blood to loud agonised cries
I'm pushed into hell
from between Mother's thighs

Torture is harsh and immediate
at such a tender age
as the Midwife slashes my lifeline, in a gory second stage
Mum's nine months of discomfort
forgotten with a sigh
burly woman in uniform
clears my mouth and makes me cry

It was SO comfy in Mummy's womb
plenty to eat with bags of room
then loosed like a hound from life's starting trap
to the human race, on my very first lap

Christened in church, a miserable place
strange man, sloshes water all over my face
while going on about some God "in his grace"

At last it's over, tears are dried
Mum's thumb in my mouth smiling with pride
glasses clinking, my frightened eyes blinking
all attending there wonder
what I must be thinking

Wake early next morning not at all happy
crying my eyes out wearing soggy wet nappy
bathed, cleansed, sweet powdered posterior
ready for jabbing, against mumps and diphtheria

Totally dependent, the first few miles
in a haphazard world full of paedophiles
pain a plenty awaits me anon
between my constant enquiries
as to where I came from

The years march on one by one
some remembered with tears, when parents passed on
their batons of wisdom for daughter and son
to improve on wise sayings left in their wake
"Resist getting angry" if kids irritate
ignore you when speaking, break the odd plate
and if disrespectful they answer you back,
respond with a hug, don't give them a slap

They need love and patience, for as long as it takes
on the long road to wisdom
paved with first time mistakes

Life's bad enough so don't be divisive
as do terrorists, keep our country in crisis
innocents killed by the black-hearted ISIS!
uneasy truce with the IRA!
man stabbed to death in bar-room affray!
Each hour's filled with bad news, day after day

If you're lucky or otherwise to have lived a long life
struggled to get through the sadness and strife
scarred by illness, survived surgeon's knife
repaid the mortgage, buried your wife

Is there really this forgiving host
up there with son Christ, and a Holy Ghost
to greet me beyond the finishing post?
I can't be sure, I'm hard to convince
that we'll share the same Heaven, peasant with Prince
I refuse to believe it and with certainty guess
if there *is* such a place
we'll surely arrive, for him to assess
unhinged by gross horrors and traumatic stress

It's almost over, I've had some good runs
as a devout non believer I'll stick to my guns.
'cos I firmly believe after popping your clogs
there's no such a place where a God catalogues
only us humans, not insects and frogs

Life concluded, over and done
remembered with love by daughter and son
then forgotten completely
when they're passed and gone.

Together at peace all the family dead
on top of each other like in a bunk bed.
Ran the race, did the best I can
an out of the betting also ran …
It doesn't matter, everyone wins
absolute absolution, no matter their sins.

The good are quickly forgotten
along with their deferent days
the bad long remembered legends
for their wicked nefarious ways.
Lie where the sands of time
part to embrace, cracked blistered foot
tired wrinkled face.

Don't worry on hearing the starter's gun
for a winning rosette's pinned to everyone.
On reaching the peace that's Oblivion.

Well as you've probably gathered after reading that, I'm not one for piety in any way, although I was in the early years given quite a thorough grounding by my dear mother in the protocol of Church procedure. I also vividly remember the ritual bedtime prayers with me and my older brother kneeling either side of the chamber pot, hands clasped together, eyes tight shut, asking God to bless by name each and every member of the family, which took a quite considerable time.

FIRST IMPRESSION SYNDROME
(Or the young duck effect)

This poem illustrates the dangers to the newly-born of a window left open in a labour ward, especially at daybreak.

Mum and dad were so excited, that early April morn
by the arrival of another son, their second to be born
every bird residing, on this half our blacked out sphere
sits waiting in good vantage, silent on a tree
to welcome one more infant day
and coincidentally *"me"*
the rising sun creeps in the room
chasing away stale, colour-less gloom
Cloud flickered sun-sent golden rays, miles in millions long
raise the heads of dormant life, rouse sleepy birds to song

Un-comfy on the baby scale, I begin to whimper, whinge and
wail
but being born at break of day
in the last few hours of April, just before the first of May
immediately I'm aware of through open window, amplified.
A cacophony of whistling by a host of birds outside
indelibly imprints, onto my tiny little mind

All about were giggling, as I chirruped in distress
stern faceted ward Sister, standing stiffly in starched dress
gropes for a rational reason with an educated guess

"There is recorded evidence" said she
and continued, deeply thinking
recalled from the past a similar event, via the vaguest of an inkling
That *"The birthday sign of Taurus is logical reason for us*
to not expect of the thousands born
everyone to be perfect and flawless.
A few could be influenced, nay, scarred for life!!
interrupting, a heightened dawn chorus."

Back home now, Mum works a routine
into which we quickly settle
for I was an awkward baby built,
for the testing of parental mettle.
Dad searches walls, woken yet again
for the nursery light at two thirty am.

Not summoned by a human
what you'd call conventional sob
more akin, to a bubbling kettle
whistling on the hob.

I ascribe my notoriety
to an eclectic bunch of tuneful friends
in thousands of different variety.
Parliaments of owls, covers of coots,
doles of white doves, a building of rooks
living and laying, eggs in spring nests,
farmers consider some, serious pests.

Most can fly free, as do you and me
sharing the sunshine with insect and bee
robins and sparrows abound in small lots
thousands of starlings, murmurate in large flocks,
others in cages, sing songs looking pretty.
Little or fat, blue green or black.
The family word when referred to each bird
is the colloquial prefix of
"Dicky".

This tragic event you have just related to yourself was one of the worst health and safety risks to have gone unanticipated during the formative years of the newly created NHS hand picked anomaly spotting team, recently redundant from Bletchly Heath, after the cessation of world war two hostilities. No more information, because of its sensitivity, can be released. All whistleblowers will be dealt with severely.

THE GOOD LIFE

This poem is dedicated to Tony Naylor who once lived in our Sheltered Scheme and whom I never saw with anything other than a smile on his face (till now?). Though I'm sure knowing what a gentle soul he was wouldn't take exception to this lighthearted biography of himself.

A neighbour of mine aged ninety three
of whom many friends concurred to agree
no nicer a guy could there ever be
devoted Christian, his everyday function
was surrogate Pope in Middleton Junction
walked to Church up to three time a day
assisted priests in every which way
counted out biscuits and shots for communion
washed sinks full of pots, from last night's Mother's Union
this good kind gentle God-phile, altruistic naturelle
prayed non stop for his fellow men, the sinful ones as well
God (he hoped) was grateful, for his work up there in Heaven.
On his knees from dawn till night, inclusive twenty four/seven

Came a time he fell gravely ill
beyond the help of Doctor or pill
pale of face through cracked dry lips
kin gathered heard him say
    "Throughout ninety years of devotion
    and time spent as amateur Lay
    I've served the Lord unerring, all my life and still
    accept this dreaded moment, to be God almighty's will."

The workman-like Priest mutters quietly, last rites in repetitive
way
scatters a few drops of water, for a life completed that day.

God meanwhile in Heaven
phoned his Pope at the Holy See,
declaring
    "I'll have to watch it in future
    this guy's more religious than me"
he simply oozes goodness and likely in future to be
a worrying threat to the prospects of our Trinity's Gang of
Three
he's a hater of globalization, our progress to world integration
and worst of all I hear
wants restrictions on other than British up here
his articulate cunning rhetoric, to gullible throats brings a lump
puts me in mind of that carrot topped twat
misogynist Donald Trump

So if you're looking for contentment on eventual demise
it's like going down to the woods today
you're in for a big surprise.
If there really is a Heaven, existing back-side of the sun
don't believe in all that hearsay
a new regime's begun
God's been deposed, in a Coup d'etat.
Now our Tony's Cock 'O' The Run.

Tony was really born in God's image, my opinion tells me he was an identical clone quite capable I bet, of sending plagues down, but not the malicious get your own back sort. Take for instance if the proper God had infected all his children with carbuncles, Tony as vice God would have immediately blanketed the Earth with a bread poultice despite the certainty of having to face his master in full wrath later. How good is that?

HARD TIMES

This is a pre-Christmas poem recalling when our Great Britain ruled one fifth of the earth together with a third of its population and all the seas surrounding everywhere else. When life for the ruling class was an overflowing cornucopia of excess and you got four dollars to the pound. But mercifully short for the deprived stunted working class majority at the far extreme of the social divide. HAS THERE REALLY BEEN A RECESSION SINCE 2008? (never noticed it myself!)

When the man of the house in the old days
either died or lost his job,
his dependents were put in the workhouse
or went thieving to make a few bob.

The same thing happened to our Dad,
turned up drunk and got sacked from the Mill
but life didn't appeal in the workhouse
separation was part of the drill
so instead we were took in by Granddad
Son Fred and his wife Aunty Jill.

On arriving that day late at Grandpa's
Mum tearfully said through a frown,
"It's going to be a bit of a squeeze
in a tiny two up and two down."

"This is no time for tears now dear Daughter,"
said her Dad on the dust covered floor,
"when the Cockroaches saw you lot coming
they packed up, and moved in next door."

There wasn't much room to begin with
specially time for bed,
Mum and the girls shared with Aunty Jill.
While I squeezed in between Grandpa,
me Dad and sweaty feet Fred.

Choking fog, diphtheria,
curtains and beds, bug infested,
complicate life even more-so,
on top of been born pigeon chested.

Everyone self-medicated
with dubious potions to treat
dozens of different ailments
in efforts to gain some relief,
from the perils of everyday problems
soothing the redness and pain
inflicted on us by our Teacher
with his long thick black knobbly cane

One of the cures for example,
viewed now with some disbelief
was a daily teaspoon of water
in which Grandma had soaked her false teeth.

The provenance supporting this treatment
with the passage of time is obscure
but we think we now have the answer,
it's an *immune supporting* cure –
only effective if carefully made
from a God fearing, aged mature.

These days, when we die, are much better,
you're frozen till there's a day,
they find a cure for whatever
killed and made you that way

Now if given that choice when I was a boy
I would've been "put down" and froze,
to await better times like at Christmas
for a motive quite odd you'd suppose.
When we'd each and all, get a large chicken leg,
instead of the Parson's nose.

There's at least one consolatory fact to having lived in those
hard times, and that was to be thankful for not having been
born a hundred years earlier. Or today.
Have you Sinners noticed though, that God through his
kindness made it so that the harder life is, the shorter it will be?
Halelujah!!

SLEEPING BEAUTY

This is a modern version of the fairy tale about the wicked old fairy who put a curse on the King's new born baby daughter because she wasn't invited to the do. Which resulted in the Princess and her whole Court having a hundred year kip until a handsome young prince came along awakening her with a kiss and to claim her for his bride.

Whether they lived "Happily ever after" or not, I don't know, because in this version their initial beginnings contrary to the original story were quite embarrassing.

I'll spare you the first part of the story, and we find the prince approaching the princess's overgrown castle.

The brambles parted the prince upped and started,
toward the castle door
Glancing aback had a panic attack
tempered with sweaty palm fear
as the re-growing thicket and slumbering pickets
dechanced a retreat to the rear

Furtively creeping by fast asleep servants,
and comatose palace guards,
mutters,
"This fairy tale method of finding a partner
is intensive and so very hard
Was alright I suppose, in days of old
when Knights were bold
and computers, a far off invention."

"Remember" to update the Monarchy
was one of the old King's intention
So going on line, will be simple and fine
a fat equerry butts in to mention.

There are huge selections, ... in the "Date a Bird" sections
With girls of a mind, optimistic to find
something better than ... poor peasant grafters.
Dreaming all day they'll be carried away
by a "well minted" Prince
'swhat they're after.

"I'll do that anon, but for now carry on"
said he with unwavering duty
and on lifting the latch ... his breath he did catch
at the sight of this sleeping beauty.

An attendant advisor,
helped take off his visor
as he got himself down on one knee
and with lips puckered up – for to steal a kiss –
thought ...why not a couple, or three?

But after the first ... her eyes opening wide
looked at her suitor and through running tears cried
"I'm distressed and cannot reciprocate
as I should ... to your tender advances
for there's more than enough ... other stuff on my mind
to indulge in your lust provoked fancies.

Please forgive ... if I seem disrespectful
bordering on the remiss
But I've just been asleep for the past hundred years –
And am bursting for a piss!

Ah those were the wild under developed days when everyone
lived within walls, the style of anti-social existence we are all
retrospectively (at least in this country) striving toward a world
where chivalry was more than just passing folk graciously
holding toilet doors ajar for easy access.

OURS IS A NICE TOWN OURS IS

This is my personal tribute – and I'm sure the rest of Middletonians will endorse the sentiment expressed – to a team of unpaid volunteers who after months of hard graft have gradually transformed the Borough's grot spots with triumphal culmination: from "Ugly Ducklings" to "Beautiful Swans".

In a Council community building
next door to the Hare and Hounds pub
therein gathers a group of Middleton-philes
assembled to do the town good.

After a two to three hour gestation
seeded by everyone there,
came a smiling pronouncement from Paula
in her capacity as chair
that tonight on this cold winter's evening
a unanimous vote in the room
had welcomed the newly-born healthy
Middleton Borough in Bloom.

Tracey and Jan on the Council's behalf
pledge their wholehearted support,
while Pat and Lisa's *Saint Martin's Gang*
just give it a little more thought.

Davina speaks to Keeley
in convivial light rapport
benignly watched over by Vicar,
the Reverend Martin Short.

Volunteers Ros, Jan and Zoe,
Catlin, Chris, and Tom
impatiently wait for springtime –
can't wait to get it on.

Jill of Youth Liaison,
as soon as the meeting ends
takes written notes from the minutes
to impact on her immature friends.

Heather, together with Julie
concentrating with eager intent
listen to Lee, the purser
guess-timating the cash to be spent.

It's now high summer
we're rushing around
unprecedented sunshine bakes the ground
everyone frantically on the go
reviving plants with H2O

Anomalous pressures to cope with,
by far exceed one or two.
Then there's the first World War's anniversary
Have we bitten off too much to chew?
It's not all the time easy going
the path's been occasionally rocky,
stumbling over minor disputes for instance,
like the Hanson Street poppy.

Lifting rubbish from gum pock-marked paving
till late in the afternoon
perspiring profusely about the Borough,
under a merciless sun since June.

As cigarette butts quickly pile up
on the footpath without Wetherspoons.
Our mission is nearing completion
and the resultant social cohesion
saw the magnificent barge at Slattocks
sail in for its first summer season.

Beautiful floral features
hang from pubs, cafes and inns
along squeaky clean environs
absent of wheely bins.

It's getting close to judgement day
when adjudicators, touring the town will say
is it deserving of a *yay* or *nay*?

A miserable nay, or an excellent yay
will be met in an equivalent way
with unanimous empathic humour.
So, no matter the outcome
let's have three GREAT BIG CHEERS
for the **UBIQUITOUS
MIDDLETON BLOOMERS**.

If you don't already know, Middleton is a small town in a huge conurbation insulated between Manchester, Oldham and Rochdale by an ever decreasing green belt slowly vanishing under developments of unwanted warehousing and industrial sites doomed to lie vacant like the ones from a previous age. This is why 'logically thinking' Middleton In Bloom was created to compensate in some way for the loss of the natural boundary, by moving it into the streets with some success as the past two years have shown: a silver medal was awarded with our first effort in 2017, then in 2018, silver guilt. And in future years? Who knows? Onward and upward. Middleton is unique in that twice a year the homeless hold a flag day for us.

CLEAN AS A MAN CALLED DAVID

Living by one's self has its advantages, for instance you have the unopposed power of pleasing yourself in whatever you do. In what could be described as a most delightful super selfish altruistic free zone.

There is though, the need for a high degree of relentless self discipline to ensure and maintain acceptable standards, now that you have to iron your own shirts.

This is the story of of one such person's successful resurrection after sliding down the "Can't be bothered" pit of degradation.

Stuck in the house it's Easter again
can't go out 'cos it's pouring with rain
skies clear up, rainbow brightens the day.
Dying April, welcomes blossom filled May

Should I sit in the garden, or laze on the grass
take an excursion with my pensioner's pass?
But the seats on the Metro are too hard a ride
sod it I'll stay, and do nothing inside.
Air the bedroom open the post
breakfast spent sucking at two rounds of toast
couldn't finish them off, fed pigeons the most.

Gummed down a bowl of Special K
pots in the sink, from a week yesterday
watch clouds re-gather, then randomly spray
oh what *a miserable f'kin day*

Pants need pressing, there's a hole in my shoe
hundreds of jobs, can't be bothered to do.

Am I getting scruffy
haven't shaved yet today
does it really matter?
Don't get out much anyway.
Time to make my mind up –
do I go, or should I stay?

Must admit I've neglected
the habitat where I dwell
Don't get as many visitors now
I wonder, do I smell?

I'll have to get out of this rut I'm in
my muscles are gone, losing weight very thin
heart's palpitating, incontinent bladder
unnecessary useless
as a carpetfitter's ladder

This rapid decline I must halt and contain
build up my body, and physique to regain
confidence, what-ever, keep virile and sane.
I'm sure feeling better, is worthwhile the pain.

The resultant reward, of running for fun
was the bolstered-up cheeks, of me skeletal bum

A restless bundle of energy am I,
from ugly bug chrysalis, to new butterfly
symbolic of power, in an athlete's vest
four inches off stomach, transferred to my chest
not still for a minute, don't ever rest

The bathroom is a temple
where I worked, achieving my goal
with exercise thorough but gentle
thrown out, all the cheap toilet rolls.
And to Andrex have lately upgraded.
No longer pathetic and jaded
head held high, walking tall
velvety Andrex hangs on lavatory wall.

Who'd have thought I could agree
that taking advice from a kid on TV
would bring such a change, stimulate me
this upright, virile, dissipate free
steely framed, muscle bound, fit as a flea
de-clinkered, re-lifestyled, re-graded.
Bum Andrex polished, morphed into be
"Clean as a man called David"

YOU CAN'T PLEASE EVERYONE

On a rubbish strewn corner of Middleton
armed with secateurs bin bags and broom
Ros and Jan clear litter
for this year's *"Borough in Bloom"*

Joined by enthused residents
refreshed with biscuits and tea
continue their voluntary clean up
on behalf of you and me.

Uncovering an old rusting street sign
at the edge of the tidied plot
they thought.
It's a century gone since world war one
and in case we might've forgot.

Ros, by way of her hobby
paints the sign a coat of white
emphasising a painted red poppy
to locals' and passers' delight.

This tiny colourful symbol
provokes passing minds to remember
the eleventh hour of the eleventh day
when they called a halt to that bloody affray.
One hundred years since
come November.

The people at Highways completely aghast
act out of character, very fast
circulating this round robin copy
"If we can't get at them for breaking by-laws
we'll have them, for being too soppy"

Please! … leave the poppy, to its silent work
jogging present day minds to remember.
Let it go on and flower
till the hundreth year's past
at the eleventh hour … of the eleventh day
on that cool Autumn morn next November.

Councils are certainly not sentimental when it comes down
to one hundred year anniversary remembrances as you will
have gathered after reading of their dogged intransigence in
refusing to bend slightly, a highway by-law, broken by accident
because no one was aware of it anyway. Pity they don't react
to public opinion as swiftly as parking tickets are metered out
here in.

"Rip 'Em Off" Rochdale

MICHAEL

Reading this poem at my son's funeral was the most emotional and upsetting experience I've ever been tasked with.

On a bright frosty day at Foxall Street,
early nineteen sixty three
A child was born name of Michael
to Margaret and me

Memories come flooding back
when the world was vibrant alive
optimistic for the future
our family complete at five

We'd already been blessed with two beautiful girls
but because of a pill,
his Mum to be
"inadvertent" omitted to take.
Must admit now, that baby Michael
was a happy, but unplanned mistake

He hated school, loved riding in cars
an intense all to frequent, pain in the arse.
But he settled down and finally found
through music he could succeed
be an ace guitarist,
the very best of leads

Spent hours alone self teaching
by himself in long noisy sessions
mastered the art of music
unaided without any lessons.
At his ultimate peak of perfection
he travelled the world wide and far
to us he was a legend –
a brilliant shining star

The last gig is over, the bright lights are dim
each one of us here will remember him.
He's played a last encore, for every fan
downed his pint, loaded the van.
for the long journey home,
where you can,
rest easy tonight.
Mister music man.

Michael is my late son who provided me with the moment every parent dreads but does not expect. Dying before his time. Given the choice I would have preferred the short straw for myself, than suffer the heartache a too long life can bring.

FIRST AND LAST NIGHT

You've all heard the Shakespeare saying "All the world's a stage" on which we all briefly appear before moving on. This poem is a whimsical summary of the events surrounding the existence of a random group performing in the repetitive play we call life.

Luckily being married to, and encouraged by his wife Anne, Shakespeare became England's greatest writer, which begs the question:

Would he have been so successful had he been married to a woman like Nora Batty?

WILLIAM SHAKESPEARE DIED 23/04/1616 AGED 52
52 DIVIDED BY TWO = A PAIR OF ALPHABETS

To quote top playwright Will Shakespeare
remembered this four hundred years
from among his much hackneyed sayings
there's a couple that spring to mind here.
One's about Cleo's lover,
wanting to borrow his countrymen's ears.
And "The world is a great big platform
on which everyone appears."

Where infinite streams of young newbies,
in the steps of forgotten has beens
act their socks off seeking perfection
stealing scene after scene.

The rest, according to talent,
cast in minor roles
support the leading actors,
like paralysed telegraph poles.
Then after the final curtain
distraught in belated hindsight
regret not working hard enough
on a no second chances, first night …
mediocre performers, wincing to catcalls and names
exit their lime-lit once only, fifteen minutes of fame.

Circle and stalls filled to overflow
with restless lost souls in measured limbo
each brings a notebook and pencil along
to see and record how and why they went wrong.
Curtain rises, "on this real not pretending"
epic production of
"LIFE WITHOUT ENDING"

Enter stage right handsome young blade
tall, narcissistic, aloof
falls head over heels for a shapely blonde
flowering away in her youth

Two comparative strangers, Daddy's daughter,
Mummy's son
drawn together by natural selection,
metamorphosed into one …
together at last the two of them, coiled in a lovers' embrace
settle down to propagate, continue the human race.

Detached from the merry gathering, Best Man's tacky pun
nature in deadly earnest, for the lovers lots of fun,
pre-marital caution set flippantly aside
frees double backed Devil's fingers
for an unprotected ride

Early evacuation/premature ejaculation
disentangles fits all sizes, missionary position
Satisfied groans, clashed with unfulfilled screams
bring to a climax act two's final scenes

Act three scene one, many years on
blessed with five children: four girls and a son.
It's now just the two of them, kids married and gone
genetically programed to follow them on.
Earthly task over, husband and spouse
sit waiting for death in their echo-less house

There in the shadows of a once vibrant home
watch again, their condensed transition
from young love, to Darby and Joan
super eight colour movies,
bounced off magnolia walls
revitalise faded moments, far beyond recall,
on this oft travelled fifty-year journey,
from springtime through summer, to fall.
Stories one for each milestone over and over retold.
Falling tears at each anniversary,
trace progress from Paper to Gold

Act three death scene
His pestle is limp her mortar is dry
the play's almost over, it's time now to die
tears falling free from first nighters' rouged eyes
blur the last moments of.
Real life demise.

~

A MESSAGE FOR THE DYING (That's all of us)

If you've lived your life to God's template,
on the afore-mentioned theme
been a regular Church goer, with a record squeaky clean
God'll let you slip away painless, before catching 'owt obscene.
Large incremental advances
will up your status, to "special mates"
so put an extra fiver on the Sides-men's copper plates

~

A MESSAGE FOR THE DEAD
Rumours abound of a new idea, the Holy Ghost is trending
there's up for grabs a million pound prize
for those clever enough ... to invent or devise
"LIFE WITH A HAPPY ENDING"

BAINES

A friend of mine Tom Baines who is now sadly deceased was required to move down south where his job was newly located. We continued to exchange Christmas cards and more recently emails, of which the one below is a sample of what men in certain age groups write about. He being a right of centre Agnostic, and me a die hard atheist indulged in many light hearted verbal rants on the subject. The following letter is a typical theory of mine in reply to one of his examples, regarding the probable scheme of things.

Hi Tom.

Found your thoughts on royalty and religion most interesting, and I wholeheartedly agree with you on every point made. Royalty in its present form can be compared to a long standing crime syndicate gone legit' who's basic philosophy during early beginnings was give me what you've got or I'll hit you over the head!

Religion is a fairytale dream of the masses born of the oppressed human condition, that interwoven with life's already established natural hazards proves to me , God and Heaven are invented myths perpetuated throughout time by the illogical superstition that *"There has got to be something better than this"*

Happyness brought about by modern inventiveness is killing religion while at the same time upsetting our earths temperate balance. Redundant places of worship are transformed into residences and supermarkets. Religion is trying to modernise by the acceptance of present day practices that would have not long ago, meant death to the perpetrators. There are so many contradictions that it's almost impossible to arrive at any conclusion but one. That the only true fundamentalists have absolutely no connection with humanity. They are the creatures who since the biological period began have stuck rigidly to the original basic principles necessary for their survival.

Don't know about you Tom but I'm a great admirer of Richard Dawkins, he has satisfied my curiosity of things spiritual, and during the process re-enforced my atheist status.

The universe in my opinion, is more chance than planned, there are countless more millions died than survived on this hostile flying sod. The whole of nature's delicate balance is a mere fluke of kindly circumstance constantly in flux, fine if left to what we call nature, but threatened with premature *"life extinction"* at the hands of mankind's clumsy exploitive husbandry. Progress is not infinite, breaking out from fundamentalism in our case, is quickening the pace to extinction.

Life comes and goes on earth, but the basic principle of our universes eventuality remains unaffected?
Tom. Doves lay more eggs than Hawks to compensate for losses at the hands (tallons) of their fellow fundamentalists.

Keep it under your hat Tom, I think I've stumbled across

the meaning of life. "Hurtling through space from one big bang to the next!"

Life in all its diversity "from microbes to men" who having evolved overtime surviving successfully by eating each other on the now rotting bits of debris, racing from the last disaster toward the next is just one tiny part of an infinite regeneration process.

Not unlike Brexit, racing thousands of miles per hour to an uncertain destination. From whatever our tiny planet used to be attached.

Happy New Year Tom.

Also by Ken Eaton-Dykes

I Know Where I'm @